Vancouver

Vancouver

Compiled by Photo/Graphics

Published by

**Whitecap Books Ltd.,
Ste 1,431 Mountain Highway,
North Vancouver, B.C.
V7J 2L1**
and

**Natural Color Productions Ltd.,
2500 Vauxhall Place,
Richmond, B.C.**

© Whitecap Books 1982
ISBN 0-920620-33-7

Printed in Canada

The City of Vancouver

In 1792 Captain George Vancouver came to the Pacific Northwest region in search of the Northwest Passage. He mapped and surveyed the area that is now downtown Vancouver, giving various parts British names. He returned to his native England little imagining that in less than one hundred years his name would be immortalized in that rugged wilderness.

Sixteen years later, following the course of the river that today bears his name, Simon Fraser arrived in what is now Marpole. He was searching for the Columbia River, and having determined that this was not the Columbia, and confronted by hostile Indians, he turned back in disappointment the same day. However the area was opened up by these overland explorations, and the arrival of the Hudson's Bay Company, and later the gold rush, began the influx of white men and the beginnings of permanent settlement.

For approximately the next sixty years the Western part of the Burrard Inlet was largely ignored. Granville, as it was known, was little more than an appendage to New Westminster, and seemed destined to remain so.

With the coming of the railroad, the importance of

Granville was ensured, and in 1886 it was incorporated as the city of Vancouver. Almost immediately it was razed by fire, and the city fathers, undaunted, set up city hall in a tent. It was at this time that the land that is Stanley Park was set aside for public use, an act for which Vancouverites and visitors alike must be eternally grateful.

Shipping increased to meet the railroad, and Vancouver soon became Canada's main west coast seaport. Although Vancouver is less than one hundred years old, an infant among the world's cities, this mood of expansion has continued, until today the Greater Vancouver area is made up of Vancouver, Burnaby, New Westminster, West Vancouver, Port Moody, Richmond, Coquitlam, Port Coquitlam, Surrey, White Rock and Delta. This area makes it the third largest city in Canada, after Toronto and Montreal. With a population of 1,100,000, it covers an area of 1,412 square kilometres. Furs and gold no longer motivate people to come to Vancouver, but development continues at a rapid pace. As well as being a great seaport Vancouver is a centre for the ever-expanding industries of British Columbia, and continues to attract growing numbers of tourists.

Opposite: Modern art at Robson Square.

Above: Robson Square at night. In the background is the old courthouse, which is at present being renovated and restored to house the Vancouver Art Gallery.

Following pages: Coal Harbour, Stanley Park, and the North Shore.

Opposite: The steam clock at the corner of Water and Cambie streets. In the background, the revolving restaurant atop the Harbour Centre.

Above: The Hotel Europe in Gastown. Since the late sixties, street and building renovations have converted Gastown, the oldest part of the city, into a major commercial and tourist centre.

Totem Park (*below*) is just one of many areas in the 1,000 acres of Stanley Park. Surrounded on three sides by English Bay, the Gulf of Georgia, and Burrard Inlet, Stanley Park is only a few minutes walk from downtown. Within the park are two lakes, floral gardens, a zoo, the Vancouver Aquarium, and an 11 kilometre (7 mile) seawall promenade. Founded in 1889, most of the park remains unspoiled.

Joggers on the sea wall in Stanley Park.

Cricket match at the Brockton Oval in Stanley Park.

Polar Bears at the Stanley Park Zoo.

The Killer Whale show at the Vancouver Aquarium.

Opposite: Fruit stall at the Granville Island Public Market. The Market offers a variety of fresh produce year round, much of which is produced locally in the Fraser Valley.

Above: Sailboats at Granville Island. Once a little-used industrial area, Granville Island has been developed into a centre for the arts, complete with restaurants, retail stores, theatres and galleries.

The pool at Kitsilano Beach is a favorite spot for local residents and visitors during the warm summer months. The name Kitsilano comes from a famous Squamish chief named Khatsahlanough.

Beach Avenue and the Vancouver Aquatic Centre overlooking English Bay in the West End. With some 40,000 inhabitants living in only 7.7 square kilometres of high-rise buildings, the West End is one of Canada's most densely populated areas.

Opposite: The Lion's Gate Bridge during rush hour. The drive through Stanley Park's tree-lined avenue and on to the bridge with its exhilarating view of the harbour and the north shore mountains, is one of the most spectacular in the world.

Above: The Lion's Gate Bridge with the city in the background. The bridge was officially opened in 1939, and today it is still the major artery connecting Vancouver with North and West Vancouver.

Opposite: Queen Elizabeth Park and the Bloedel Conservatory are situated atop little Mountain in the geographic centre of the city.

Upper: Lily ponds at the Van Dusen Botanical Gardens.
Lower: The rose gardens at the main entrance to Stanley Park.

Following pages: Downtown Vancouver at sunset.

Opposite: The Orpheum Theatre, built in 1927 as a vaudeville theatre. A concerned citizens group raised the money to save it from demolition in 1973, when it was completely refurbished and became the home of the Vancouver Symphony Orchestra. It still houses the original wurlitzer organ, one of the few in North America.

Located at the entrance to False Creek, in Vanier Park, the Vancouver Museum and Planetarium occupies the site of what was once a Musqueam Indian Village. Although the planetarium revolves around its daily shows in the 'Theatre of the Universe', it also offers various exhibits in the museums.

Next to San Francisco the city of Vancouver boasts the second largest Chinatown in North America. Its citizens jealously guard their ancient traditions, bringing the culture of the Far East to Vancouver.

Every year the community celebrates the Chinese New Year with a parade. Participants include many local residents in traditional dress, and the mandatory firecrackers and dragons. No matter what time of year, there is always something to do, from browsing in the many stores to dining at a first class restaurant with a cabaret.

Young participants in the Chinese New Year parade.

Taking inventory at one of Chinatown's restaurants.

Opposite top left: The Museum of Anthropology, University of British Columbia. *Top right:* Salmon barbeque, Vancouver Sea Festival. *Bottom left:* The Pacific National Exhibition parade. *Bottom right:* Craft fair, West Vancouver Community Days.

Above: Every year for two weeks Vancouver hosts the Pacific National Exhibition, featuring the midway, trade and consumer shows, agriculture, sports, and major entertainment stars. The P.N.E., as it is popularly known, is the fifth largest fair of its kind in North America.

Ships at sunset, English Bay.

The Sea-Bus crossing Burrard Inlet.

Opposite: A jogger soaks up the last rays of sunlight on the seawall near Siwash Rock. Local Indian legend tells that Siwash Rock was once a man named Slay-kay-ulsh who, because of greed, was turned into stone by the Gods.

Lost Lagoon was given its name by the Indian poet E. Pauline Johnson, who spent many hours exploring the little tidal inlet of Coal Harbour in her canoe.

Opposite: Sailboats leaving the shelter of False Creek for the waters of English Bay and the Gulf of Georgia.

The sea is a natural and integral part of life in Vancouver. As well as various sailboat races there are two major festivals, the Sea Festival and the Vancouver Sun Salmon Derby.

Following pages: Third Beach in Stanley Park.

Opposite: The Hotel Vancouver, finally completed in 1939 after a seven year delay during the depression, was opened for the Royal visit of King George VI and Queen Elizabeth.

Above: Granville Street, one of Vancouver's main thoroughfares, takes its name from 'Granville', the original name of the city.

43

Opposite: Grain from the Canadian Prairies is transported by rail to the Alberta Wheat Pool terminal. From here it is shipped to China, Japan, the Soviet Union, and many other countries.

Above: Scenes from the Port of Vancouver. The port is Canada's largest Pacific terminal, and nearly fifty million metric tonnes were shipped from Vancouver last year. Cargoes vary from lumber, grain, and pulp to coal, copper, sulphur, and potash.

Cyclists pause to admire the view of Stanley Park.

Silhouette of English Bay from Stanley Park.

The Capilano River as it leaves the canyon.

The Capilano Suspension Bridge.

Opposite: The Nitobe Memorial Garden. Since its dedication in 1960 the garden has attracted thousands of visitors with its two examples of Japanese garden art. There is a small teahouse where on occasion elaborate tea ceremonies are held, and a larger theme garden, which represents the journey of life and the varieties of nature.

The University of British Columbia campus is situated at the tip of Point Grey peninsula. It is the largest university in the province, and offers various degrees ranging from sciences and arts to medicine, education, forestry and commerce.

Opposite: British Columbia Ferry leaving Horseshoe Bay enroute to Vancouver Island.

Above: Sailboats in Fisherman's Cove, West Vancouver.

Following pages: An aerial view of Lighthouse Park, West Vancouver.

Opposite: The Lynn Valley Canyon

Above: The Point Atkinson Lighthouse, West Vancouver.

Opposite: The Grouse Mountain skyride transports up to 100 passengers on each trip to the summit of the 1,250 metre (4,100 feet) mountain.

Upper: Ski mountaineering on Mount Seymour.
Lower: Downhill skiing in Cypress Bowl.

Photographic Credits

Jurgen Vogt   Pages 4-5, 6, 11, 15 (above), 17, 20, 22, 29, 30, 34, 35, 37, 38, 43, 45 (below), 49, 61 (below).

Marin Petkov   Page 7, 18, 19, 23 (below), 24-25, 32, 33 (top left), 42, 52, 53, 59.

Duncan McDougall   Page 27, 58, 62-63.

Michael Burch   Page 10, 23 (above), 33 (below right), 50, 55.

Ed Gifford   Page 14 (below), 21, 22, 28 (above), 28 (below), 31, 33 (below left), 33 (top right), 36, 49, 51, 54, 60.

Vlado Matisic   Page 16.

Manfred Kraus   Page 26.

Gunter Marx   Page 15 (below), 39, 44, 45 (above).

Dane Simoes   Page 14 (above), 48.

J. R. A. Burridge   Page 61 (above).

The photography in this book was compiled from the files of Photo/Graphics, a division of Herger & Burch Agencies Limited.

The color separations were made by Tri-Scan Graphics Ltd., Vancouver, British Columbia.

The book was printed and bound by D. W. Friesen and Sons Ltd., in Altona, Manitoba.